THE ATELIER PROJECT

CONVERSATIONS ABOUT CREATIVITY

Dedicated to my first child. A new creative adventure!

The Atelier Project

CONVERSATIONS ABOUT CREATIVITY

Edited by

Molly Miltenberger Murray

CONTENTS

ACKNOWLEDGEMENTS

I'd like to give thanks to the creatives who contributed to this book and to the creatives who have poured inspiration into my life. A special thanks to my husband, Gordon, for his design work and for his balance – he enables and inspires my creativity!

INTRODUCTION

Rage – Goddess, Sing the rage of Peleus' son   Achilles, Murderous, doomed, that cost the   Achaeans countless losses... Begin, Muse.[1]

Creative thinkers have always wondered: where does creativity come from?

The Greeks attributed creative insight to the Muses, the divine daughters of Zeus and Mnemosyne, the goddess of memory. The Muses gave their grace only to the deserving. Steven Pressfield, a contemporary guru of creativity and author of the books, *The War of Art* and *Do the Work*, is convinced of the mysterious nature of inspiration and attributes it to the 'Muse'.

---

[1] Homer, *Iliad*, trans.Robert Fagles (New York City: Penguin, 1990), l.1-7.

Other names for this mysterious force might be the Unconscious, the Self, the Quantum Soup. Whatever it is, it represents the unseen dimension of Potentiality that is either within us or beyond us. It's where ideas come from.[2]

Like so many beautiful things, the creative force remains a mystery. This book is a celebration of that mystery.

One thing about the conundrum is clear: the Muse doesn't reward slackers. Inspiration is a combination of this elusive concept of artistic vision and honest sweat. Pressfield explains that if you put in the effort, the Muse will put in the vision.

> Is this magic? A miracle? No, it's common as dirt. It's how creativity works. We show up. We do our best. Good things happen. This is the intersection of hard work and inspiration.[3]

This intersection between muscle and Muse is the creative process. And that is something that we can most definitely explore.

I've spent years burrowing into it through books and personal experience and conversations – so many conversations with so many different people in so many different places. This book is a continuation of those conversations; a gathering of collective experience. It's an

[2] Steven Pressfield, 'You as the Muse Sees You', 9 Oct. 2013, *Stephen Pressfield Online*, http://www.stevenpressfield.com/2013/10/you-as-the-muse-sees-you/
[3] ibid.

exploration of creativity, and I hope that it's an illumination of the way that creativity thinks and works.

An atelier is a concept with powerful connotations. The word is rooted in *astella*, the Latin word for 'a splinter of wood'. It moved into the French language as *atelier*, 'a woodpile', and branched to designate 'a woodshop or a workshop'. The term now carries the connotation of an artist's studio, an intentional creative workspace that splinters inspiration and fosters invention. In an atelier, creative ideas are both born and brought to life. It's an area where an artist uses the space, lighting, and color of the room like media: an atelier is a canvas for creativity.

Like an atelier, this book is an intentional space to explore and inspire creativity. I hope that you keep the conversation going.

The best and only thing that one artist can do for another is to serve as an example and an inspiration.

– Steven Pressfield, *The War of Art*

CREATIVE

INSPIRATION

Annie Higgen

Poet

TO S.

To call you my muse

and by mere use of two words

project us

to higher grounds

feet no longer touching

unearthed yet all too human

desperate groping for flesh

in the dark and the silence

when you say little

and I spread the sheets

Oversimplifying you

and me

and the motion of reaching

of wrapping and tearing

the blank page the blunt nib

like a dance

all too easy

yet an ache in every muscle

overstretched

fatigued

You are round

my paper

a mere surface

I wrap you in it

from every angle and still

leave you naked

bare

dissatisfied

your cubist third eye

staring back at me.

Javier Suarez

Yarn Owl

Musician

INTERVIEW

A phrase, something I'll hear, will inspire me – it's funny how little it takes to get a song going. A friend ended his email with 'stay in tune with the moon'. Now it's a song. You take a spark and put it together with other little sparks and it goes on its journey of growing and becoming.

When I was living in an apartment last year with a friend, we had a whole wall dedicated to 'yarn art', which is also called needle painting – basically, pictures that are constructed with yarn, in frames: the kind of thing one always seems to find at Goodwill. It strikes me as one of the most beautiful but under-appreciated art forms. My favorite piece in our collection was of an owl sitting on a branch. Hence, 'Yarn Owl' comes from this lovely art form.

Interview with the editor. Stereopathic Music. *2008.*

Sean Ogilvie

Musée Mécanique

Musician

INTERVIEW

I'm from the San Francisco Bay Area. I would frequent the Musée Mécanique, a museum that's full of turn-of-the-century mechanical toys, when it was at the Cliff House, this really cool nostalgic place on the Pacific Ocean by the Sutro Bath ruins. It had this really old feeling: there was a lot of history within that really cool nostalgic place. The penny arcade pieces were always very inspiring.

When Micah and I started making music a couple of years ago, the music just had the feel of a music box: kind of folk, kind of all these different pieces of all these different songs – different pieces, coming together. I like the idea of antique music. We like certain timbres, we like certain colors, we like putting them together. Tonight it felt kind of like a circus act. I was afraid I was going to fall off the stage.

Interview with the editor. Stereopathic Music. *2008.*

Barry Lategan

Photographer

INTERVIEW

Girls. I like photographing the world of women. I observe the decorating ways of women. I describe their world as *thaumaturgy* – a word that means miracle-working. Women work miracles with fabric, colours, textures. I like looking at women. Women are magical. You see, you girls – look at the colours you wear compared to guys. We just cover ourselves, but you decorate yourselves. You're like butterflies.

When I worked in New York I had three female assistants; they were more multi-tasking than men – you know that, they are. When I was in *The Tyra Banks Show* the crewmen were standing around arguing about the equipment because it was faulty. The girls stood together in a group and said 'We've got to do this; we've got to do this; we've got to do this. You do this, you do this, and I'll do that.' Girls solve problems. Men tackle problems.

My mother was a dressmaker, so perhaps that had some influence. Photography was a hobby for me in my younger years, and I had to do some military service – that was part of the system. While I was serving in Germany, I started photography again as a hobby. I went back to South Africa, where I grew up, and my mother, upon seeing this hobby of mine, mentioned it to a neighbor who knew a photographer. I said, 'But this is my hobby!' I walked into his studio and I saw around the walls all these pictures of beautiful women in fashionable clothing, not glamour pictures, but fashion pictures. He said, 'Would you like a job?' And I said, 'But I have a hobby; this is my hobby.' He said, 'You're a lucky man who can make your hobby your work!' So here I am, thirty-five years later.

South Africa is the country of the natural origins of life. I grew up on a farm, where the trees were taller than the buildings. I grew up without telephones, without television. I grew up with nature. Krishnamurti believed that life originated in Africa: you feel that with the animal life, the plant life, the tribal people.

I grew up in a time like you had in America once of segregation, severe segregation. Eventually I left Africa when I was a young man and when Mr. Mandela went into prison. I was amazed by the speech he made after he had been in prison twenty-seven years. They made a statue to him here last year and he made a speech that did not condemn a single person in his tributes, whereas the Prime Minister and the Mayor of London condemned everyone. Mr. Mandela said this statue is not just for one man; it is for all men, against segregation.

I've photographed a few jazz musicians; I've photographed Dizzy Gillespie, I've photographed Jerry Mulligan. I'm inspired by Chopin, classical music, and opera. When I was a young man, seventeen years old, in South Africa, I saw an advertisement for an opera, *La Bohème*. I'd never been to an opera. I went by myself, aged seventeen, and I came out on the street and I was in tears. It was the first time in my life that I had experienced ecstasy – the difference between sexual and emotional ecstasy: I was totally aroused to myself. You know how we all seek ourselves in what we do. This music inspired me; it was tremendous. I think opera was probably my first arousement. Opera these days is like

11

our world is – our world is, can I say, a potpourri, a mixture, a labyrinth of influences.

As Krishnamurti said, 'Each of us carries the imprint of the friend met along the way and each carries the trace of each for good or evil, in wisdom or in folly, each stamped by each we pass, lit briefly by one another's light, thinking the way we go is right.'

Interview with the editor. Personal blog. 2009.

Matt Bishop

Hey Marseilles

Musician

INTERVIEW

We share an appreciation among all of us for the beauty that can be accomplished in stringing together waves of eclectic acoustic instrumentation.

Some of us lived in places like Bahrain, Australia, and New Caledonia while we were growing up. I'm sure that has something to do with the references in our songs. I've never been to Rio, nor have any of my Hey Marseilles compadres as far as I know. I have been to Calabasas. I have never been to Tallahassee. I have been to northern bays, though never jumped from their cliff sides. A desire to be someplace else, as well as an interest in capturing that place lyrically, is what the music seems to be saying to me.

My favorite book is *Confederacy of Dunces*. The same appreciation for the absurd that compels my love for that novel must also be at the core of my ability to spend weeks in a tour van with six dudes.

Interview with the editor. Personal blog. 2010.

Colin Herd

Poet, Fiction Writer, Critic

FROM *VASARELY MUSEUM*

The lights keep going on and off

split second thought:

an elaborate trompe l'oeil

Zebras appear and disappear

I try to grab you over

but you've already seen them

(and not seen them)

We're the only visitors

making it easy to dash about

2nd, 3rd, 4th looks at

favourite paintings

Eyes bulging

nervy Op-Art pulse

and the sun

and it's our last day

Abstract sphere bursting forth

you ask if I've ever seen

the film *Alien*?

We're debating if Vasarely's a pop artist

during the documentary:

"screened courtesy of MTV"

Also in the film

Vasarely wears glasses

hardly a surprise.

CREATIVE
ODYSSEY

Marcas Mac an Tuairneir

Poet

AND

We cannot agree
On the flow of the wave,
We cannot grasp
The teasing wind.

Some leave marks,
Expecting an illustrious future,
Like a long-term vigil on the horizon,
And a mirage over the mountains
Like the hope
The advent of the tongue's Messiah.

Against them, one hears
The call of another throng,
And the crack of the whip.

Under the cairn, while they advocate
The past;
They bury vowels
Under the glacier.

And the other lot,

That would re-write history,

With suffixes,

That would raise sound,

Moribund,

Like Jesus to the weak hand of Lazarus.

But we all travel,

In our patchwork carriage,

With it's sunken, whizzing wheels,

Propelled by scattered intention,

And all the contention,

Chastising our children and their questions.

Jo Young

Creative Writer

WHAT WAS MISSING

Have a look on the internet at what 'Rushing Woman Syndrome' means and you will get a picture of a harried woman, probably a professional, probably with some children, a mortgage and a burning English-girl need for approval wherever she goes. Hermione Granger aged 39.

Checking her e-mails at red lights, surviving on wine, coffee and carbs. Never shifting the baby weight, yet always exercising. Keeping a spotless house. Well, maybe not spotless, but pretty regimental. Multi-screening in the evening. Wine at hand. Doing a job her father would have done by day and doing everything else her mother would have done in whatever time is left.

A meditation app was supposed to be the solution. But when she found herself writing 'meditate' on her to-do list somewhere between 'clean car' and 'post stuff on EBay' she admitted she had missed the chance to acquire transcendence. A visit to the doctor for irritable bowel and occasional panic attacks was a good move; a liberating chance to talk about the iron bands on the chest and the tightening furnace in the intestine. She never wanted medication, but she knew she needed more than that big box of Laxido.

But you know what? She's fine now. So what changed? What came along to temper that brain that raced along like the mind of a lunatic? Starting everything, finishing nothing. Existing in a soup of cortisol, adrenalin and constantly revised resolutions.

Well, she found the courage to answer the doorbell that had been buzzing, constantly for twenty years.

She started to write.

She wrote and she showed it to other people who wrote.

And they didn't laugh or shrug.

They called her a writer and they smiled and suggested things.

It became her job.

It became her occupation because it occupied her. Like an invading force; it settled and bred with what was there.

It became what she does. Whatever else she might do, writing is what she does and now she has permission to prioritise it. To put time aside for it and to let it dwell inside her.

Writing. Creating like never before.

She is busier, but she is more fruitful.

Her family like her more. Her jeans fit better. Her sleep has deepened.

But she still multi-tasks. Oh boy, does she!

When she is walking the dog, she takes the time to trace the knots of the tree branches around her and tries to describe them for a poem. She notices how the overflow from a Victorian reservoir could provide the lethal terminus for a tragic character. She looks up the name of a flower that only blooms for one day in June to add a convincing layer of fact to a short story.

When she is in the supermarket she listens to the words and the vernacular of the shop assistant. She finds comedy in the fish that kiss on the counter. She invites her toddler to choose his own dinner. And she joins him in a picnic of black olives, pizza, jelly and grated carrots.

There is inspiration everywhere. Stories litter the parks and poems pour from the exhaust pipe of the car front of her. And it makes her realise that she will never be wasting time again; she will always be writing or thinking about writing. Panic subsides, urgency decreases. She has found what was missing.

Brandon Summers

Helio Sequence

Musician

INTERVIEW

Benjamin and I met when we were teenagers growing up in Beaverton, a suburb of Portland. Like a lot of suburbs the 'culture' wasn't very colourful or varied and the feeling was very insular and restricting. It was just a lot of malls, televisions, box stores and cars. I was really restless growing up there, thirsty for more than sitcom entertainment and hanging out at malls. Music was really an escape and salvation for me.

When Benjamin and I met we realized that we both loved music of all sorts. There was a really strong local scene in Portland in those days – bands like Hazel, Thirty Ought Six, Pond, and Elliott Smith's first band, Heatmiser. We'd go downtown to watch shows and it was inspiring to be a part of things. We really began branching out and exploring new types of music; we were always excited to share new bands that we'd discovered with each other.

Our music all began with a family picnic when I was 16. Without my knowledge I had been 'booked' by my mother to play at a big family get-together at a very strange, campy amusement park outside of Portland – kind of the Coney Island of Portland. The only problem was that I didn't have a band and I had less than a week to write songs and get one together! I talked to Benjamin about it and he had the great and (at that time) eccentric idea of making a band with sequenced keyboards. He had been working on a keyboard project for most of the year and wanted to try mixing some of those ideas with a real band. So, along with his younger brother Paul, we sat down and wrote three long instrumentals that clocked in at over 10 minutes each. After we played the picnic we all agreed that we had really hit upon something different with our mix of organic and electronic elements – a different angle. That's how Helio Sequence began: almost as an accident, a happy accident.

It all evolved from there really. We spent the next few years writing songs and beginning to add vocals into the mix. It was all a whirlwind of influence because we were learning about a whole world of music so quickly and ingesting so many new ideas. The more spacey rock, English bands like My Bloody Valentine, Ride, and Lush were really inspiring, and also American bands like Bowery Electric, Labradford, King Black Acid, and old sixties rock like The Kinks and The Beatles. It wasn't until 1999 that we pulled it all together and put out our first EP, *Accelerated Slow Motion Cinema*.

Our sound has evolved over time from the 'wall of sound' approach of our early stuff to a 'songwriting' approach, but there's something at the root that has remained constant.

We're both fascinated by the texture and the feeling of sound. The visceral experience of sound is as important as the song itself.

I've come out of the experience of losing my voice as a stronger singer than I would ever have been otherwise. When I lost my voice it was really rock bottom, a really bleak and vulnerable time with so much self-doubt. It was much more than a simple physical loss of voice. Everything was called into question: my future, my past. But working back up from nothing allowed me to see things in a different light, to leave behind old habits that had constrained me, and to work on new things that open up the possibility of songs. It was a new beginning. I look more deeply at a lyric now and listen to all music with a different ear than before losing my voice.

There were so many amazing books that I came across during the time that I was getting my voice back. Reading is a path that I continually walk down. One book always leads to another somehow, whether it is directly referenced, recommended to me, given to me as a gift, or stumbled upon by chance. I wouldn't say there was one single book that changed my life but they all change the way that I see things. Looking back, the book that probably had the biggest effect on me was Ralph Waldo Emerson's *Essays*. In high school we were assigned to read 'Self Reliance', and it blew my mind. I read all of the rest of his essays religiously.

The music of Helio Sequence is an ever-evolving idea. We're inspired by the love of music; it's an endless world. I have a simple hope that the songs and sounds find their way into people's lives.

Interview with the editor. Email. Stereopathic Music. 2009.

Jennifer Trovato

Photographer

EXPOSURE

I've taken photos for as long as I can remember. I've had dinky point-and-shoots, a few film cameras, a mid-range Digital SLR, and now a full frame DSLR. I started taking photos of my family and friends, and branched out into friends' weddings, babies and numerous other word-of-mouth projects. It's been a slow and steady path of creativity throughout the years, but looking back, it's amazing to see where this passion has taken me. I love that photography allows me to be included in others' lives in such an intimate way, documenting their sweet moments as a family, on a wedding day, with their newborn, in their own creative space, or even their own creations.

My creativity not only manifests itself through my photos, but also through reaching out to people and just putting my talents and myself out in the world. I find that I lose *most* inhibitions when it comes to reaching out to people over email, so I've been able to make connections with people that I never imagined I would possibly be able to work for let alone speak to. I pointed to the work in my small portfolio and shared my desire to grow, and I've been given opportunities to reach and stretch my technical and creative abilities. Through allowing myself to work for nontraditional payment (trades, exposure, experience), I've been able to make connections and receive the exposure I need to get more lucrative jobs and projects. Finding people that are looking to grow themselves seems to be a great way to partner together and be able to provide talent while receiving opportunity.Thinking outside of the box when it comes to how you do business ultimately affects your work and the brand you are presenting. The world is so small now; it can never hurt to just start a conversation with that person you think would never read your email.

To me, creativity means being okay with looking like an amateur to stick out from the crowd a little bit. It is trying something knowing full well that it may be a total waste of time right now, but will be completely worth it for your own path later. Creativity in ways both artistic and practical has brought me to a place in my life where I can do projects that are inspiring and challenging, with the ever steady hope of an upwards growth in my craft.

Caleb D. Ackley

Photographer

STORY

The story of my life as an artist begins a few years back, so let's rewind the tape. Some very simple things encapsulated art to me while I grew up: black-and-white film, my sisters' collective artistic talent, my parents' love of good literature and story telling.

I picked the camera up out of frustration instead of love for the art form. Ever since our family camera bit the literal and figurative dust on the beaches of Southern California, we, as a family, had not been able to document any of our collective outings. There were years' worth of pictures that had not been taken, and, when I was thirteen, I had had enough. I saved and bought my first camera. A Canon Powershot, I believe – a battery-draining friend that would stick close to my side for the next five years. In the early stages, photography was just a means to an end, a stepping-stone to catalogue and re-live experiences. Nothing more.

As I got older, however, I began to take my camera to document the time that I spent alone and the places that I went, as well as the time I spent with my family. Before I knew it, things that I saw begged to be captured as well. Texture in a weather-beaten fence, the way the wind constantly reshapes the trees, the glorious expanses of wheat-fields – I gladly responded to their calls.

About the same time, a passion for stories, especially stories of dedication, love, perseverance, and self-sacrifice, was slowly but surely growing inside me. My romantic bent I attribute to Christ's saving work in my heart, as well as to the works of C.S. Lewis and J.R.R. Tolkien – both authors that my parents were faithful to read to my siblings and I when we grew up. When I came to know the Lord as my Savior in the fall of 2009, I was shown that He, as Creator and Redeemer, was the Author of the ultimate love story: the story of Christ's passion and love for the church. I found romantic stories entertaining and engaging before, but now, with Christ in my heart, stories of love became essential and full of joy.

Soon after that, I moved from rural Northern Idaho to Southern California. I began to pursue photography professionally and, before I knew it, I was in the middle of my first wedding season. Several friends were tying the knot, and the event designer that I interned for assigned a wedding to me. I relished the work that I did and thrived on the energy of the day, but, as I dove into post-production, I had to come to terms with a pivotal fact.

The kind of work I was doing was not even close to the artistic standard that I hoped or envisioned it would be. I grew frustrated, knowing that my work was sub-par, but not knowing how I could possibly improve it.

Fast-forward six months. I received a message from a photographer that I'd come into contact with during my internship. I had great respect for him as a photographer, and in many ways, it was his type of style that I wanted to shoot. He asked me if I wanted to start meeting with him. I responded with an astounded (and disbelieving), 'Yes'.

I took a hiatus from my own work and concentrated solely on learning from my friend. For a year, he went through every last detail in my work and critiqued it. While it was humbling much of the time, it was absolutely essential to my growth. By the end of that year I had finally begun to output the level of work that I had always envisioned. I had an established portfolio, and I began to build up a clientele.

That brings us to where I am today. I'm not full-time quite yet, but I am planning to be able to make the jump in about two years.

Stuart White

Creative Writer and Biology Teacher

FIRST LOVE AND MOVING ON

As a conscious process, creation is an evolved idea, stemming from the human primordial instinct to procreate. Biologically, we are programmed to produce new variations of ourselves for the continuation and advancement of our species. In many ways, that's how I view writing: to create a story is to create a variation of myself. It's been said for a long time that a little piece of the artist's own soul, personality and morals is infused into each fictional character. The need to put a variation of self into fictional situations and to experience emotions through those situations is a powerful draw to creation.

My overwhelming urge to create comes from my desire to entertain. I want people to enjoy something I've written. Validation as a writer is secondary to the possibility of making a reader smile, cry or experience something which removes them from their world into mine, even for a moment, a second.

The stimulus to start writing came from an injury that I sustained in 2010. Training consumed my life for about ten years prior to that. Rugby, the love of my life until I met my wife, took every waking thought and dictated every action. I chose my occupation because it suited my training and game schedule. I socialised fairly exclusively with those involved in rugby. Writing has always been there, thrust deep into the background as an unhealthy obsession, a lusty teenage crush that lingered into manhood. After my injury, I turned to the deeper, rewarding love of the craft that has since devoured me.

Now, I do little else. Read, write, work, sleep. My caffeine intake has quadrupled. My sleep is restless and riddled with frustration at my inability to use a comma, properly. My cortisol levels are almost always elevated after a working day with hormone-saturated teenagers. They dissipate as I sit at the keyboard and crunch the keys. You might call it therapy, you may call it enjoyment, but for me it transcends emotion. Writing isn't just something I do. It's now a part of me.

Now we are months into the Creative Writing programme at the University of Glasgow, and my process and routine are as ingrained as the habit of brushing my teeth every day. Write for two hours. Read for one. It doesn't seem like much, but that's the minimum. It's not uncommon for me to crawl to bed sometime in the wee hours, having been unable to stop myself from writing or reading – but most nights I'll settle for a page or two of decent writing. Creation is hard work, more graft than craft for me. As a self-confessed non-literary writer, the effort is doubly tough.

Without a doubt, participating in the writing group on my master's course has been a major turning point for me in terms of my creative development. The encouragement, insightful advice and feedback I've received have been invaluable. The knowledge that I'm not alone, that others do the same thing night after night, is an enduring comfort, and one likely to sustain me for the many lonely years ahead.

I mostly focus upon producing something in line with my own reading tastes. After all, that's the idea, isn't it? To create stories that I love and to keep writing until I have nothing left to say.

Nichola Deadman

Creative Writer

WHERE THE FALLING ANGEL MEETS THE RISING APE: WHY FICTION MATTERS TO ME

I struggle with fiction.

There, I've said it. My whole life I've wanted nothing more than to write books: fun, *excellent* books that blast into people's minds like literary rockets, provoking empathy and sparking imagination. The kind of tales that drag people around the campfire of the spirit and join us in the ancient and visceral communion that is the sharing of a story.

But I struggle with fiction.

This probably has a lot to do with a number of things that happened to me when I was nineteen. The climax: I met a very cynical young man at the bookstore where I was working at the time.

I asked him what he was looking for. 'I don't know,' he said. 'Something interesting.' And I suggested some new release, some fiction best seller that I was probably keen to read myself.

'No thanks,' he said dismissively. 'I don't like to waste my time on things that aren't true.'

I probably just froze. I'd misunderstood him somehow, surely. I remember trying a few more times to probe this idea of someone who just *didn't like fiction*, but he remained unmoved and a little sneering, as though liking fiction made a person weak and a bit delusional.

This made *no sense to me at all*. Books had always been part of my life. According to family lore, I taught myself to 'read' with an audiobook of *Puff The Magic Dragon* well before my second birthday. By the time I entered primary school I found the junior section of the school library laughably easy and got special permission to take books out of the mysterious senior section.

My parents did not restrict my reading in any way whatsoever – a fact for which I am eternally grateful. I was a voracious and indiscriminate reader in a house full of eclectic reading material – my mum's big fat romance novels and my dad's manbooks (I have read *shameful* amounts of Wilbur Smith and Louis L'Amour), leftovers from my much-older siblings' university careers (*A University Anthology of Poetry*, Simone de Beauvoir, Athol Fugard) and the old books that came from nowhere: James Herriot and Gerald Durrell and Roald Dahl's 'grown-up' short stories (no one forewarned me that the man who'd produced *The Witches* and *The BFG* had also written *My Uncle Oswald*. I loved it anyway).

Most of my pocket money was spent on books – libraries didn't cut it. I wanted to possess my literature. I'm a re-reader and don't like to give books back in case I might like to read it again in future. I still remember the glorious day I went into the Central News Agents and bought my first Terry Pratchett book, *Interesting Times*, because the cover looked, well, interesting, and the back sounded funny. That single book sparked a lifelong love of his writing, which has probably shaped my personal philosophy more than any more serious texts.

Even better were the high school years when my beloved English teachers loaned me books from their personal collections, introducing me to Margaret Atwood, Rohinton Mistry, Salman Rushdie, Barbara Kingsolver, John Fowles, E.M. Forster – books that opened my mind to bigger issues and made me more socially conscious.

And hand-in-hand with my love of books went my love of writing. I have always known I wanted to be a writer, although for most of my life it was something I thought I'd do... at the end. After I'd had a real job. After I was properly qualified. When I had something to say.

I pottered about with writing for years, never wholly able to think of it as a potential career. But in my final year at high school I managed to win both

Poetry and Prose categories in my school's annual writing competition. I still remember the magical moment when my English teacher read out my short story to the class – I remember the hush, and my cheeks burning with embarrassed pride, and the silence when Ms Cator finished reading. 'That doesn't sound like it was written by a student,' she said, sounding awed. 'It sounds like it was written by... you know, a real writer.'

I don't say these things to boast. I say them because they meant something huge to me: *that people liked my stories.*

And then I turned nineteen, and blundered into a series of situations that seemed perfectly designed to destroy what small confidence I had in my writing. My mum's death left me feeling vulnerable and in too much pain to create. At university I was surrounded by people, it seemed, who were older and smarter and knew more than me. I realised I had not believed the stories of my religion for a long time and was not particularly bothered about it. And if studying politics makes you wise to the world, it also makes you aware of how much of it is a lie: how history is twisted and philosophers make things up and even countries exist only because of how much we have historically invested in the ideas of governments and borders.

I came to distrust narrative.

So I stopped writing, and I stopped reading. It didn't *mean* anything to me. When the young man in the bookstore told me that he thought fiction was a waste of time, I thought, 'he's right – why waste time on things that aren't true?'

I graduated and moved to Japan to teach. I lived in a little town in the mountains for my first year. I didn't speak enough Japanese to make meaningful relationships with people in my town, and so I lived in silence for that year. It was peaceful and weird and terrible – I got horribly depressed and did things like wander through the town at five o'clock in the morning listening to Coldplay on my iPod. I became a Zen practitioner and a vegetarian and then I stopped because it wasn't really me. I felt incredibly free.

But all these empty hours started me reading again. My next job, a year later, was incredibly unfulfilling, and in my endless desk-bound down time I read and read and read. I read two hundred and fifty-six books over the course of about three years. I kept a list. I read fantasy and crime novels and nonfiction and children's books and Japanese literature. I read rubbish and I read brilliant stuff, and it made me feel human again.

And one day, on a whim, I decided to do NaNoWriMo – if you don't know what that is: every November, thousands of people around the world compete not against others but against the demons of self-doubt and procrastination to write a 50,000 word novel in 30 days. Doing that successfully means you've won.

I didn't expect to win it the first year I tried, but I did.

It felt *good*.

The following year I quit my job to work part-time and focus on writing, which was unproductive but soul-healing. I watched a lot of TED talks, got pretty good at photography, and won NaNoWriMo again. I started thinking about doing a Masters in Creative Writing but still I wasn't sure I had enough to say, enough talent, enough experience.

I couldn't let go of the idea though. Encouraged by friends, I signed up for the MLitt at Glasgow, gritting my teeth and flapping my arms as I filled out the admissions forms. I signed up because I liked the look of the programme and only Googled the University of Glasgow on the last day of the admissions window, then felt oddly comforted – *of course* I wouldn't get in; it's three hundred years older than my country. I'd shot way above the mark.

I got in anyway.

It's been brilliant. For the first time in my life I have a cohort – other writers who take me seriously. I love my schoolwork and desperately wish I'd had the courage to pursue this years ago, because there's nothing so fulfilling as doing what you love. I'm getting to know myself as a writer again, building up the fledgling confidence and learning how to deal with criticism and rejection (but also enjoying a bit of the other end of the stick).

This was going really well until a few weeks ago, when during a conversation about fiction, a friend of mine shrugged and said, 'I prefer to spend my time on things that are real.'

Chills down my spine. All the old insecurities came up and I spent a very dark afternoon wishing I'd opted for a Masters in Linguistics instead and Googling articles on 'why fiction is relevant', to convince myself I suppose.

In my search I came across the scene from Terry Pratchett's *Hogfather*, where the character Death talks about how humans need the little fictions – the stories, the fairy tales – as practice, so that they might believe the bigger ones – justice and mercy – that give meaning to our lives. 'To be the place where the rising ape meets the falling angel'[4] – the clash between the desire to be something better and the disappointment that we are not.

Fiction is a way to understand that we are not alone in our questions and doubts. It's a way to explore the forces in ourselves we cannot articulate because of shame or fear or simply because we don't have the words yet. Throughout history we have communicated these nameless things through legends and folklore and other, grander stories designed to inspire and explain. Stories are part of us, whether we want them to be or not.

For me, once I understood this, I understood also that I wanted to take my place as a storyteller. I don't claim to have answers, but I understand now that it's not answers I want, but empathy, imagination and a shared experience. And at last I understand why. I still struggle with fiction, but from now on I want to struggle to tell my story well and to share it with others. I've stopped questioning whether it's worth it. Maybe someday I'll write the story that will help me figure it out.

---

[4] Terry Pratchett, *Hogfather* (Gollancz, 1996), 422.

CREATIVE
INSIGHT

Seth Brown

Why I Must Be Careful

Pianist

INTERVIEW

Why do humans exist other than to get away from the necessity of making food and shelter? To escape that excess and find time to do something else... art.

Interview with the editor. Stereopathic Music. *2009.*

Emma Jane Kimmell

Visual Artist

CONVERSATION

Just about everything inspires me to create. It's hard to credit just a few things. Sometimes it's my outfit, sometimes it's the sun and flowers outside, sometimes it's a song and sometimes it's the environment. I like to be able to sit down and create a masterpiece at any moment. I've really been working on putting myself into new situations to create because I want my creativity to be mobile and not dependent on anything.

One of my fundamental beliefs is that I should leave things better than I found them and I do my best to carry that into all parts of my creative life. With my students, I leave them more confident, self-assured of their artistic ability and inspired to continue to create. Picasso said that 'All children are artists. The problem is how to remain an artist once they grow up.' My job is to make sure that they are confident enough to grow up willing to share their work with the world. There's no such thing as too much creativity. With my personal art I create beauty out of small things. Everything I touch I try to leave my creative mark. I leave my customers with more colorful walls, my friends inspired to create and the world with more beauty.

I came from a line of interior and graphic designers. I used to spend a lot of time in my Nana's interior decorating shop and have always had a creative eye. I became interested in painting in high school and even though I was not very good I kept at it. I decided to become an art major and thrived in that environment. I knew it was my calling and the major I needed to be a part of. I began sewing and designing my own clothes, worked long hours in the studio and began spending most of my time in coffee shops sketching. I started my project 'Sketch a Day' around that time in March of 2011, and I've been doing one sketch a day since then – which comes out to about 1,460 days of sketching! It was that project that improved my skill, allowed me to express my creativity, and find my style. I began looking into opportunities for art shows and I had my first show at age 18 in Spokane, WA. I moved to Seattle to pursue art, got a job as a children's art instructor, and haven't stopped doing art since then. I had a great solo show in Seattle where I sold about 75% of all my work and I realized that I needed to make a business out of this.

My life is such a creative one that it's not too hard to stay creative. I spend time everyday working on my daily sketch and am always working on new designs, commissioned pieces, home décor, and fashion. I follow artists, designers, fashion bloggers and photographers on Instagram and try to hit up the local art museums every couple months.

I love my creative routine. It's when I feel most alive and most myself! It usually starts out with a clean desk. Then I break out the French press, the headphones, the paint, the markers and Sharpies, and whatever else I can find. I just start creating. Sometimes I know what I want to make; other times I just flow and end up with something completely unplanned. Hours later, the apartment is pretty near destroyed. Paint has usually been splattered everywhere, drawers opened and emptied out, and crumpled drawings are strewn about on the floor. It's quite a sight. The worst part is cleaning it up, but I have to get it clean for the next creative session. When I'm not home or I'm in a new place for sketching, I still pop in my favorite tunes and get working. Sometimes I spend long periods of time people watching, looking for something to spark my imagination.

Creativity has brought me to my calling in life. I'm meant to teach and inspire young minds and share my art with the world. It's what makes me feel fulfilled, what wakes me up with the drive to tackle the day. It's brought me to start my own business to sell my work online. Eventually, it'll help me to open up my own art studio where I can teach young artists.

I don't know if there is such a thing as a perfect piece of work. I think art can come close to perfection but I don't think it'll ever touch – and sometimes that's a hard realization for me. I can always see the flaws in my work and I have a hard time letting go of pieces and selling them. But I think that's also what makes art special: it shows the creative hand behind it. When someone wants to buy a piece of my art, that's perfection to me.

Justin Ringle

Horse Feathers

Singer, Songwriter

INTERVIEW

I have been singing since I first started playing guitar when I was 15, but it is a song-by-song thing. Sometimes the feeling of an experience or an event will get me started to come up with a melody. It often just happens. I will play everyday and things will come out and I will have to work backwards to figure out where the inspiration is coming from.

I have no larger motivation than just to please my ear and the will to make something new. I think that when that motivation changes the music could ultimately suffer, so I try to keep that part of the process simple.

'Horse feathers' is an old saying meaning nonsense or rubbish. It's something I heard my grandfather say growing up. I like how it sounds kind of antique.

Interview with the editor. Email. Stereopathic Music. 2008.

Lovísa Elísabet Sigrúnardóttir

Lay Low

Musician

INTERVIEW

I think having two very different family heritages [Sri Lankan and Icelandic] has helped me to be a little bit more open to different things in my surroundings. I was born in London, grew up in Iceland and have family all over the world.

But musically, I'm not sure: most of my influences are from here in Iceland, some, of course, from all over. My father never listens to music from Sri Lanka so I had not much influence from that part in my childhood, but in recent years I have been listening to music from Sri Lanka. I've found a lot of beautiful songs and singers that have become addictive.

Growing up in Iceland inspired me very much: the nature and the landscape, the people, the bright summers and dark winters. It is a small community. If you don't know everyone, you probably know someone who knows someone and so on. Musicians and artists are helpful and the listeners are loyal and very supportive. I think I always say that my favorite place is Iceland, I love that it is so small but still very big. It makes me feel safe and snug but never claustrophobic.

I hope I'm not being too cliché, but I would say that feelings inspire me to create music. The need to express feelings, the need to share feelings, the need to relate to others, the need to get over feelings, the need to evolve feelings: the need to feel something.

I have many favorite books. But there is one Icelandic writer that makes me cry and laugh at the same time, and that is something I like doing. Her name is Kristín Ómarsdottir.

Someday, I want to buy a house in the countryside and grow my own veggies, kids and love.

Interview with the editor. Personal blog. 2010.

Bart Budwig

Folk Musician

CONVERSATION

Life. Interactions with natural beauty, with created beauty, and with other humans inspires me to think – which often ends with a strong desire to create; it might even be a requirement.

My creative life began by playing jazz trumpet and working on poetry assignments in high school.

I write to find truth and I find that I am only smart enough to ask questions. Madeleine L'Engle said 'If it's bad art, it's bad religion, no matter how pious the subject'; Flannery O'Connor said 'I write because I don't know what I think until I read what I say.'

I stay creative through long drives and good conversations; I keep musical instruments handy; I have a digital voice recorder on me for song and melody ideas; I keep goals to perform or record; I need well-written books, quiet and time to think and reflect and create. I'm most creative when I'm alone; I'm often driving or at home.

My creative routine is to enjoy something beautiful and to think about it. Then, I pick up an instrument for creating music or for writing.

Creativity has given me a strong desire to learn and to connect with people. It's given me a recognition that being wrong is okay. It's taught me that working hard and creating beauty bring great joy.

A lot of work, imagery, and a little bit of hope make a perfect piece of work.

Lisa Jane Birch

Fine Artist

CONVERSATION

I would say that work is essentially incited by thought process, imagination, memory, senses, and the other actions that take place within the human mind. I think that a lot of work is to do with reflection; it is based heavily on personal thought and mental dialogue. I'm obsessed with shape, form, and shade, the way that one abstract shape is created by the intersection of other shapes; it's a continuum.

The circumstances that I see around me and the way that I see people behave are my main influences to create. Throughout our lives we behave a certain way due to various factors: circumstance, surrounding, language, class, background. I'm always pondering why we are the way we are, and how individuals arrive in a certain place.

I'm inspired by taking long walks, by reading, by traveling, by learning from other people, by evaluating situations. I like to see the learning process as a continuum that doesn't stop: you are always taking in information even if you don't realise it. I completed my Fine Art degree in 2011, but I will be returning to university this year to study Social Psychology. I think that continuing to learn is a way to constantly feed your creative side.

I remember my mum showing me how to create an intricate pattern with a line drawing that she had seen on a show for kids. I became hooked on pattern and shape, and began to create my own alternative ways to form them.

Normally, my routine is to get up, have a coffee, read the news and then get cracking. It hasn't been easy to get the balance correct, but I would say that now I generally have a good balance between working to pay the bills and creativity.

Creativity has brought me to question more, to be less judgmental, to try and peel back my first impressions and see if I can look into a topic further; it has taught me not to take things for granted, to appreciate what I have, and to try and see the beauty around me. One medium isn't more valid than another.

Creativity comes in waves. It's up and down: some days things work, some days they don't. I go through phases; it's not something I can just switch on and do. Creativity is out of my control but I've learned to let it go. When something is not working, I simply put myself to doing something else. Being creative doesn't necessarily mean creating. Reading, thinking, drawing, walking – whatever you like to do – is just important as the actual creation itself.

For me the creative process and the idea of the piece is generally much more interesting than the aesthetic. I like to ask, 'What is the concept of this piece? How did the artist come to make it? What are the artist's interests? What are the artist's influences?' I like to know the background of the work.

The most successful work, in my opinion, is one that each viewer leaves with a different interpretation. I would say that a successful piece of art is one that touches each person in a different way.

Ian Lyles and Aaron "Rantz" Pomerantz

Weinland

Musician

INTERVIEW

In every songwriting circumstance, our motivation is always to serve the song through instrumentation and dynamic. I think our primary aim is to make records that are timeless, that you creep up on you, and in the end stay with you for the rest of your life. Plus, we like to drive around the country and play music together.

Adam had been writing music for many years and had started performing and recording under the name John Weinland. Adam and Rantz began to play music together with the kids they were working with at a mental health facility for at-risk youth. After work, they spent a few late nights playing music for fun. Slowly, other instrumentation was added. Adam's friend from Montana, Rory, picked up the bass. Alia Farah added vocals and piano in the early days. Ian Lyles brought over his drum set. Paul came in as the keyboard player. There are still a lot of rotating cast members in Weinland. We are tight with our Portland music scene pals and love to incorporate additional players when we can – we bring in big hitters like Rachel Blumberg (Decemberists, M.Ward, Bright Eyes, Jolie Holland), Laura Gibson, and Adam Selzer (Norfolk and Western, M.Ward) to make those extra bits of instrumentation sing!

The musical community here in Portland is very important to us. We have experienced so much support and friendship from fellow

Portlanders, we can't imagine trying to do this anywhere else. Portland has a good thing going right now. Not just based on the number of musicians and artists that live here, but the spirit of growth and the willingness of everyone to be helpful to one another. For example, last time we returned from tour we had a coming-home show the same night as The Decemberists, Laura Gibson, and four or five other bands that we know and love. We finished playing our set and members of all of these different groups started coming down to the bar we played. We rallied and set up a super fun, drunken jam session of Neil Young songs until they closed us down. It's an amazing experience to live in a place that provides such encouragement.

Obviously the world economic circumstance is affecting everyone, and we are certainly feeling it as a touring band. Even before this whole mess, the music industry had become a difficult environment in which to thrive, one in which the deck seemed to be stacked against the musicians and writers and performers who care about making good and honest music, who care about the art. So what do we do about it? We record a record, quit our jobs, drive around the country and take it back!

Interview with the editor. Email. Stereopathic Music. *2009.*

Kerrie McKinnel

Creative Writer

CONVERSATION

I write, photograph, knit, bake, draw for the same reasons: to create something, to capture an image or an idea with the hope that one day it might make somebody somewhere smile, laugh or cry. I'm inspired by everything and anything – a song from my childhood playing on the radio, my toddler throwing a tantrum because his yoghurt is finished, or waves breaking beneath a pink sunset.

I'm not religious. I believe that every life has value and everyone has a story to tell. I guess that is what pushes me to capture moments and memories in the way that feels appropriate.

I have always loved writing. As a young child, I started writing my own novels – they were nothing more than a couple of sheets of A4 paper with perhaps 100 words and a few drawings, but to me it was beautiful to see my own words on paper.

I keep my eyes open to the world around me. I travel and go places when I can, and when I can't, then I read, talk and listen. There is inspiration everywhere!

I have a fifteen-month-old son, so any notion of routine these days usually stretches as far as mealtimes and bedtimes. I work around him – when he is asleep, I work. If he naps for two hours, then I'll read or write solidly for those two hours. If he doesn't nap, then anything essential gets done once he goes to bed at night. I'm lucky to have a lot of help and support from my husband and from all four of our parents, so I can take a few hours off every week to allow my brain time to wander and create.

My love of writing brought me to the University of Glasgow's Creative Writing course where I have met a group of inspirational and supportive friends.

Creativity gives me an escape from the real world, a chance to get ideas out of my head and to work through them on paper, and an opportunity to escape to that beach at sunset whenever I like!

I don't think any piece of work is ever 'perfect'. There is always something that you could go back and change. You can only ever do something to the best of your ability in that moment.

I am creative wherever I have space and quiet. I would love to say that I have a wonderful little studio somewhere, but unfortunately it hasn't happened that way – there is an armchair in the living room where I spend most of my writing time. I always start with quiet, good lighting and a cup of tea. You can't go far wrong with that!

Ian Richardson

Creative Writer

CONVERSATION

What inspires me to create seems to be linked with playfulness. If you want me to dig up my creative roots and examine them, I can only do so in a playful way because I fear I will kill my creative vine and I don't believe that you can stand in your own light.

I have my own three-part plan for world domination.

1.) *Beginner: Thief.*

You may be a thief of thoughts but I don't believe you can be a stealer of souls. My blunt statement would be that 'it's impossible to copy'. If you disagree with this statement, then go away and paint a perfect copy of *Mona Lisa*. When you come back suitably chastened, sit up at the front of the class beside the teachers, ready to learn and discover your own style among your mistakes and misunderstandings. Someone once said that 'all art is self-portraiture'. I'd go along with that.

2.) *Intermediate: Master Thief.*

If you become proficient at copying someone else's style you may become famous. But you also may become known as the British Da Vinci, the Scottish Rembrandt, the Tullybaccart Andy Warhol or possibly, the (insert village name) Banksy. You need to take it further than that. Creating in the style of someone you admire should lead to the unleashing of your own creative power. In folk music, Robert Zimmerman tried to channel Woody Guthrie. He transformed into Bob Dylan. The 'folk process' of taking a melody from one song and mixing it up with the lines of another song to create a new song can take you a long way in any medium as long as you understand the medium.

3.) *Expert: Master.*

It's all been done before. If there's an original thought in the world, I could use it right now. Study all the masters that have ever lived and be inspired by their work. You have to know the rules and fully understand them all before you can break them. With a thorough understanding of any medium and its limitations, a master can create original masterpieces. When photography threatened to eclipse painting, Picasso and Braque created cubism. A camera could take a portrait, but painters could combine multiple views on one canvas. If you hear yourself say, 'I wish I'd thought of that,' you are not yet ready to become a Master.

I started writing because I realized that I wasn't going to live forever, and I set out to achieve immortality through my work.

I stay creative through research. If I have nothing to say because of creative block, it's because I've drained everything that I've absorbed about a subject. I keep my eyes and ears open.

I like to follow William Blake's routine. I think in the morning, work in the afternoon, eat in the evening, and sleep at night – but, quite often, life and creativity get in the way.

Physically, creativity has not brought me very far. I'm still stuck to planet Earth. Mentally, though, it has brought a greater understanding of how vast, fragmented and chaotic this world actually is. I read that Modernist artists saw fragmentation as an existential crisis that they, somehow, had to solve. Postmodernists often demonstrate that chaos is insurmountable and eschew closure.

Many Greek philosophers contemplated the concepts of perfection and excellence thousands of years ago. Aristotle thought that 'perfect' meant something 'complete' with nothing to add or subtract, something that had attained its purpose. Empedocles, according to Vanini, said '*perfectio propter imperfectionem*: perfection depends on imperfection.' Imperfection possesses a potential for development. I like that idea: that an imperfect piece of work inspires its recipient to become active in mind and imagination.

CREATIVE APPROACH

Susanne Wawra

Poet

ONE, TWO, THREE

A parachute mind

Takes the jump

Floats in the wind

Swims in the clouds

Braves the fall

Because he knows

He will open wide

And land safely

On his brainy feet.

Colin Herd

Poet, Fiction Writer, Critic

MR. TURNER

Have you seen *Mr. Turner*? I watched it the other day and found
the scene with Timothy Spall strapped to a ship's prow in a squall so
moving and funny. Some creative routine! He takes the *en plein air*
experience to a whole new level. I mean, he gets bronchitis because of it,
which only deepens his already profound grunt. The pace of the film
picks up right after that in an episodic fashion as if Mike Leigh's passing
round popcorn, shuffling cards or dividing out the money at the
beginning of a game of Monopoly. Scenes hither and thither - one minute
on a steamer, one minute in bed. One minute in the Royal Academy
acting like an *enfant terrible*, the next minute nearly dead. It's like that
whole loony dook episode unhinges Turner a little and from that ensuing
chaos, his fate is sealed but also he is going to create some amazing,
unexpected and experimental work from it.

So, it got me thinking: how to get that creative chaos but leave the
bronchitis on the shelf? At first, the film made me want to turn my hot
water off and make some kind of ship-like structure to strap myself in a
freezing shower and not get out for an hour or two. Until, I don't know, I
was swallowed up in some vision or realisation or something or (more
likely) gave up and recycled the structure to be used for acting out
DiCaprio and Winslet scenes from *Titanic*. But more seriously, that kind of
thing only works, if it ever works, if you have previously put all the hard

preparatory work in, which you see Turner doing throughout the film. He's always painting, when he's not grunting. Seascape after seascape; ship wreck after ship wreck until at some point he is able to become the emotional ship wreck himself and substitute for the sky this whole plateau of built-up feeling. He can only do that though because he has practiced and honed and worked so hard to get himself to a point where he can produce something that is creative (more than creative, astounding, breathtaking) and not just a wet person with bronchitis. And that's the biggest thing I learned from that film: to just put in all the hard work and to just keep writing over and over and over even if it seems like you are treading the same ground because from all of that work you don't necessarily know what's going to come of it. Oh and I also learned to brood and grunt with considerable gravitas.

Annie Higgen

Poet

TO BUILD A HABIT

To build a habit

to construct what should be growing naturally

from a seed planted deep inside

force of life pushing to the surface

for me, hard labour

like heavy bricks lain in soft uneven soil

too little mortar and stormy weather

I stand with dirty hands, water in my shoes

in the shadow of a palace someone else raised from the ground.

To get into the habit

to force by repetition what should be a flow

a steady river, subconscious urge

an outpour of swelling water, overflowing tides

I stand shivering at its ledge

naked and awkward

anticipating the breath stop shocking splash

unable to move I ponder

the slow decent with hands of water

bedewing goose-bump skin

an inch at a time

as the breathing gets heavier and the piercing pain.

I seem without rhythm

moonless without orbit or trajectory

a rogue stellar object on star-crossed passage

pulverised in the face of the sun.

I hold on to this pen

grab the edge of this paper

each word a beat

I will be a dancer in time

just practice just practice

build a habit

I'll be fine.

Sarah Palmer

Creative Writer

WHAT I THINK ABOUT, WHEN I THINK ABOUT WRITING

I'm a slow writer. Very slow. And I dither, always finding something else to research, or a new novel to read en route. But I get there in the end, and have come to realise that the slow pace, the dithering, cogitating, digesting, are a key part of my writing process.

I've been writing on and off since around 2002. I wrote during my childhood (short stories mostly, I was never a poet), and then in my teens I did some journalism, contributing to student newspapers and so on, but I didn't write fiction for around thirty years.

I like to think of that period of my life as The Research Years.

Fiddler On The Roof. 1973?

My mother took me to see this film at the Odeon, Belmont Circle. I can't remember the exact date, but it was probably around 1973, so I'd have been around seven or eight. She thought it was very important for me to see a film about my 'heritage', but didn't realise that rather than imbuing me with the same deep feeling of cultural and spiritual belonging she herself experienced, it triggered instead a series of recurring nightmares whereby Hitler comes to get me, personally.

Just the opening refrain of *If I Were A Rich Man* still has the power to bring me out in a cold sweat, and it's only been in the past year that I've been able to wear a peaked cap.

The Odeon, Belmont Circle is now a halal butcher.

Miss Rivers and Miss Bridges, Geraldine Symons, Puffin Edition. 1974.

My parents had a friend, Thelma, who worked for Collins, the publishers. She'd come over to our house a couple of times a year with armfuls of books, some of which were proofs, and sometimes they were books she'd been sent by other publishers, because this was still the golden age of publishing, before Rupert Murdoch and all that. Anyway, *Miss Rivers and Miss Bridges*, the story of two young girls caught up in the Suffragette movement, was one of the best books she brought me. Like *To Kill A Mockingbird* or *Jane Eyre*, it showed how a story can entertain and say something important about the world at the same time, and I was hooked.

It was also around this time that Thelma took me to see Father Christmas at Selfridges, and then we went round the corner to a little café where she ordered me a knickerbocker glory so tall I had to stand on my chair to eat it.

We lost contact with Thelma after my father died in 1996. I don't even know if she's still alive.

Once Upon A Star, The Bay City Rollers. 1975.

It was fortuitous that The Bay City Rollers' new LP came out in the same month as my tenth birthday, because it meant I could go to the record department, upstairs at Preedy's in Harrow, and buy it with my birthday money.

It being the 1970s there was only one record player in the house, and I had to time my shang-a-langing beween my parents' James Last,

Barbra Streisand and Kenny Ball fixes. The other thing about it being the 1970s was that our house, like the record department at Preedy's, was almost entirely brown. The *Once Upon A Star* sleeve had yellow and green on it, almost blinding me with its gaiety.

Around this time my English teacher, Mr. Morley, told my parents that my writing should be encouraged. He entered a story I'd written into an essay competition for all the schools located in the London Borough of Brent, which was linked to the Queen's Silver Jubilee. I was second, which apparently was a very big deal as I was the only state school child to be placed, and was awarded a book token, published in the Willesden Herald, and invited to the prize-giving ceremony at the Gaumont State Cinema in Kilburn which included, for some reason, a screening of *Jesus Christ, Superstar*.

My parents didn't really want to watch the film, but I enjoyed it a lot more than *Fiddler on the Roof*. Besides, I was into acting by then, and writing was forgotten.

The Gaumont State Cinema was built by the Hyams brothers, sons of a Russian immigrant baker. It is now one of a chain of evangelical churches.

Preedy's has become a Superdrug.

Can You Feel The Force? The Real Thing. 1979.

On the first Friday of every month a disco was held at the local leisure centre. All my school-friends went but I wasn't allowed to go because I had to stay home on a Friday night, light the Sabbath candles and 'be Jewish'.

My parents didn't read or speak Hebrew, and rather than go to synagogue or anything 'Jewish' like that we'd have a big row over dinner, and then watch *It's A Knockout*.

Harrow Leisure Centre is now run by a private company which runs leisure centres on behalf of local councils across the country.

I like to go to the pub on Friday nights.

Chicken Soup With Noodles, Potatoes, Peas.

Boil a chicken for an hour and a half in plenty of water with carrots, whole peeled garlic cloves, and onions. When the chicken meat is falling off the bone take it out of the broth and strip off all the meat, casting aside the bones, skin, and those knobbly bits of gristle that appear from nowhere. Meanwhile the broth should continue its happy bubbling, with some salt and pepper added. Cook vermicelli noodles, peas and potatoes separately. I say separately, but you can cook the noodles and peas together – just not in the broth.

Those with less faith in their soup-making abilities may add a chicken stock cube right at the start, but this is the action of a heretic.

Everyone gets a bit of everything, meat, vegetables, carbohydrates. Consume at times of illness or psychological stress, or just because it's nice.

Chicken soup comes in tins these days, or Tetra Paks. But people will keep adding coconut milk and Thai green curry paste to it, which isn't quite the point.

The Queen Mother's Funeral. 2002.

After graduating I worked in publishing in London for a several years, but I wanted to be closer to home in Hertfordshire when my eldest son was born. The technology recruitment company I worked for made staff cuts as the clients ran out, so in an effort to look busy, and hold on to my job as long as possible, I started writing stories again.

One of them was about people watching the Queen Mother's funeral in their office as they waited to hear if they were going to be made redundant. It was based on a true story.

It's Not Unusual, Tom Jones. Timeless.

We moved to Worthing in March 2003, when I was seven months pregnant with our third child. A couple of months after he was born I realised (because I was freelancing and didn't get to talk to grown-ups very often, unless it was about nappies or pureed carrot) that I was going mad. I dug out a few stories and, my brain sodden with hormones and lack of sleep, tweaked them a bit before looking around for local writing classes.

The ones I attended were run by Jan, a very supportive woman who encouraged me to enter short story competitions, which I won from time to time, and then to write a novel. *Dancing in the Kitchen with Tom* was the story of a Jewish widow falling in love with a vicar, who sang Tom Jones songs at karaoke bars. A few agents showed mild interest. It was funny in places, and got onto some or other shortlist, but I knew it wasn't that good, because it had been written with an eye on what my mother would think of it.

Around this time I looked again at the short stories, and how they focused on romantic love, or shopping, or shoes and thought... *Really? Is this me?* And I knew that it wasn't. It was time for the filters to come off.

Jan has moved to Dorset and now writes under a different name. She's so successful you can buy her novels in the supermarket. Or any good bookshop, of course.

My desk. Worthing, 2015.

Now I just write whatever's in my head. I don't think about 'the market', or worry if someone might recognise themselves, or if my mother will faint away at my blasphemy. In any case she's afraid she won't like my writing, and actively avoids it. I could have set those sacred cows alight a long time ago. Imagine the fun I'm going to have with them.

I still listen to Tom Jones.

Forrest VanTuyl

An American Forrest

Impressionist Americana Songwriter

A WHOLE LOT OF DIFFERENT KINDS OF WORK

I started writing lyrics because I wanted to be in a band and I couldn't play guitar. I learned how to play guitar. Now I rhyme in my sleep.

I wake up, grind coffee and boil water, pee, drop the needle on Miles Davis' *Sketches of Spain*, return to the kitchen, make coffee, check email, regret checking email, and look at mountains and/or trees when in mountain and tree-graced ecosystems. I have no breakfast except coffee and, maybe, a cookie. That's the end of my routine.

Working on a song, for me, is a whole lot of different kinds of work. It exhausts me. The end of a song is like boxing: the final stretch is like a series of jabs. There is focusing, pacing, and shouting. Sometimes a typewriter (a Remington) is involved, but less so these days. The song and its story come from the accruement of images, thoughts, and daydreams that I record in small, brown Moleskines or regular-sized black, lineless (God help me if I ever own another ruled notebook) Leuchtturm notebooks, for now. For my current project, I use scraps of paper (recycled; never new, blank paper or Post-It notes) pinned to maps of Western North America. I'm writing western songs, not country songs. Sometimes, I use hunks of butcher paper, baking paper, or (because I used to wash dishes in a bakery) sliced-open flour sacks that I pin to the wall.

I like writing on walls. I like to write while I'm standing or leaning against the wall, or from a typewriter at chest height. I pull small images from the wall scraps and notebook scraps, and I connect them into stories. I rhyme them with things they shouldn't rhyme with. I invent words. I steal lines from Willie Nelson, Bart Budwig, Woody Guthrie, Butch Cassidy, Ian Tyson, Gary McMahon, Jose Alfredo Jimenez, Tex Ritter, traditional cowboy songs, and words on the maps.

Songs ain't all words, though. A song without words is an instrumental song. Words with no music are poems. So. The chords are just the right ones. I don't have a band to work with but I like full chords, so I have to invent positions and chords to create piano chords on the guitar that sound right.

Melody? What the Hell's melody? I don't know how to write melodies. They just fall out of the sky and the chords and rhythm of the words make a net that catches the right-sized one, and I hope that it's still alive enough to do somethin' with. But writing songs is not at all like fishing. Some of the chords and melodies in my current song batch, an album-to-be in progress, are borrowed from other songs in the batch, like sisters. Some are meant to sound like an old cowboy ballad that opens with a waltz on a D chord.

Writing songs is exhausting. When they aren't exhausting, then they're invigorating. They jump up into your arms and dance with you and y'all can just hi-toe hippidy-hop honkytonk all night long.

I always try, but I never write a song I don't like, because every time I let one I don't like slip by it becomes the most popular. Little shits.

A perfect piece of work is the one that can't be fixed anymore. It just works. Some work better than others, but they've all got their jobs, and if they don't do 'em it's my fault. They work best when they haven't been tinkered with too much, and sometimes a small fix is worse than gettin' started. Sometimes though, a perfect song is the one that keeps runnin' no matter what you do to it. Bob Dylan has a lot of those.

Things that inspire me to create are trees, borders, historical injustices, the horrible things that humans do and the fortitude that gets the ordinary or the exceptional out of such places. Salvation is here on earth, as it were.

I keep working because not working is impossible. It triggers bouts of acute depression. It is something I do too often.

What is my belief, anyway? I believe Art is somewhere out there cutting holes in the fabric of the universe, Science is showing us exactly where and why those holes showed up the way they did, and Religion is what we think the holes mean to the way we live and treat each other and the earth and the trees, too.

How does that come into my art? I (try to) make shit that's beautiful, that tells a story that hasn't been told quite as much as it should, and I hope that someone hearing that story will figure out something important and beautiful, too, and that their life will be a little less bad or more good.

Creativity has taken me to Europe, looking for sanity, and to Morocco, looking for light; it's taken me to New Mexico, looking for the gritty, deathless west, and to Nebraska to drive a potato harvester because creativity wasn't paying the bills. I've written in all of those places, and more – *Idaho, Washington, Oregon, Montana, Nevada, Utah (rhymes with Me, Pa), Pennsylvania* – and more.

How do I stay creative? Today, I painted. I'm not good at painting, but I went for a hike and sat down with a little watercolor palette and started painting a rock. Then rain and sixty-five mile-per-hour winds descended on me, so I hiked down and painted trees inside and cooked beans. The nice thing about painting and cooking, and the major drawback to writing music, is that you can listen to music while you paint and cook. That's odd. I think it plays into the 'kill the thing you love' truth. But it's okay, because there will always be more love inside. Infinite Russian dolls of love.

Eat more cilantro, tequila is the new whiskey, tacos. Amen.

Susanne Wawra

Poet

PEN ON PAPER

pen on paper

i start to exist

lines melt into words

strokes shapes images

pen on paper

i am the moment

grasping the present

creating the now

pen on paper

i am alive

breathing the ink

feeling the flow

when i stop

i fade away

falling into nothingness

crippling from reality

what remains

is pen on paper

i've made my mark

i have been

Tracy Butler

Visual Artist

A HISTORY IN HOURS

My jeans were in bits. Red faced, I handed them to Carys.

I was bending down to pick up the handful of steel wool I had dropped when I felt my trousers rip – right across my backside. They had been my husband's and had travelled the world with him as he worked on oil and gas ships. The permanent oil stains on one ankle and down one leg had been gained in engine rooms. They had been repeatedly washed in strong soap powders and were fading. When he put a hole in them going down a slide with our son, he had handed them to me. Now I wore them to paint in.

I had fake fur wrapped around my waist in an attempt to maintain a hint of dignity, but fur doesn't go well with my old, greying, paint-splattered trainers. I made a swift exit from my department and arrived in a panic in the sewing room. Those jeans were comfortable. I wasn't ready to give them up quite yet.

Just a few weeks earlier I had been asked if I would be interested in working on an American TV show that is produced and set in Scotland. I am an artist with a background in theatre. I never imagined that I would be working in a costume department – I was a wildlife painter when they asked me, for heaven's sake.

Carys' machine whirred as she began to neatly stitch the rip back together in an intricate design – she was the embroidery expert after all, and I took the moment to pause and look around.

I normally just dashed in here to pick up whatever needed my attention, and dashed out. But I couldn't do anything until I was properly clothed again, so I studied my surroundings.

The room was bright and filled with waist-high tables covered in scissors, chalks and paper patterns. Enormous deep shelves holding tartans, tweeds, cottons and linens lined one wall; against another stood rails of finished costumes. Small cupboards containing threads, brocades, laces, beads and wools nestled below chaotic bookshelves. Banks of sewing machines and costume designs covered any remaining wall space. Male and female mannequins dotted the room in various states of undress, but they were unmistakably from the middle of the 18th century.

A heavily brocaded, deep green frock coat with a matching waistcoat and breeches; the exquisite wedding dress that had taken ten people three months to create and embroider; ball gowns, cloaks, and day gowns; the costume of an English army officer for a red-coated captain. Gold gleaming buttons held back the large navy blue lapels. The coat tails were opened outwards, exposing the coat's blue interior, and held in place at the sides, mid-shin height. Large blue cuffs were folded almost to the elbow. It was paired with a matching red waistcoat and breeches. The costume was beautiful. It stood out, bright red, against all the other clothes. I knew how long it had taken to knot the complicated braids that adorned the shoulders.

'Finished,' called Carys as she stood and handed my jeans back to me. 'And so's the Captain. I'll get him ready for you while you get dressed.'

I was in awe of the creations produced by the sewing room. I can do anything with a paintbrush, chalks, pencils and pens, but with a needle and thread in my hands, everything turns *very* ugly. 'He's stunning.'

'Well, he's all yours now.' Carys pushed the costume towards me.

'Thanks for the repair work.' I said, extremely grateful, and I headed, with the pristine Captain, back to my filthy studio.

I stopped briefly at my work table to grab a few necessary items and shoved on my dust mask (the kind of thing you see in World War II films), clipped it securely round my head to cover my nose and mouth, snapped my goggles into place, and headed outside through a fire door.

I placed the captain costume in the middle of a clearing, stepped back to have a good look, and took a blowtorch to it.

Did I mention that I work in Costume Breakdown?

I take those clean, beautifully-made costumes and create a history for them.

Some have become hand-me-downs worn by children that have been lovingly repaired by their mothers (heavy sanding to roughen materials and create holes, a spot of darning, maybe a touch of paint around hems and cuffs where children find it impossible to keep clothes clean). One belonged to a wealthy gentleman who had the habit of repeatedly holding onto his lapels (a gentle rubbing down in that area with a cheese grater). When buttons are too plain for the Costume

Designer's latest ideas, I make them look wooden or patterned or bejewelled with paint and glaze.

The Captain, though, was meant to have been through the wars, and his costume needed to reflect that. It needed a lot of attention.

So I took a blowtorch to it, brushed off the stinking burnt wool, and burnt it more. A wash. A dry – but not in a carefully-arranged-on-a-hanger kind of way, no, in a crumpling-the-breeches-on-the-floor-squashing-the-arms-into-creases-and-tying-them-in-place kind of way.

I spray-painted the costume, adding depth and shadow and highlight, blended scorch marks where necessary (wielding a blowtorch isn't a precise art), and finally, dulled the gold of the buttons, brocades and braids with a metal tarnisher and burnt umber paint.

Every item of every costume gets treated in Breakdown. Whites – underskirts, shirts, handkerchiefs and stocks (the pre-cursor of the cravat) – are dyed to remove their pristine glow. Handbags, hats, stockings and jewellery are all aged, their brightness dimmed to fit in with the design of the production. Boots and shoes are sanded to give them scuffmarks; the under-sole is cut away and painted to make it look worn. Then, there is the application of mud made from clothing dye, water and cat litter – don't tell the actors! Of course, mud splashes can be very, very messy and a lot of fun.

It took years to imprint a history on my jeans but in Breakdown, we create one in hours.

Marcas Mac an Tuairneir

Poet

SYNDROME

And the poems come
At four a. m.

The stacatto stanzas
And shattered clauses.

Broken bodies and bones.

A leg,
Waxy and pale
Like that of a doll.

Raw,
Weeping at the hip.

An arm,
With hand outstretched,
And none to hold.

I dread the face,

Bulbous and deformed.

The black, brilliant eyes.

The chapped, blue lips,

Parted;

In silent howl.

Yes.

These are my embryos.

The dark thoughts

That return and replay,

Like a grumbling old man.

I shout,

To drown them out.

Involuntary cries.

I cut my long hair.

I love my mother.

I didn't mean to do it.

Michelle Case

Singer, Songwriter

WRITING A SONG

Writing a song is like going for a run. Sometimes it's easy. Sometimes it's awful. Sometimes your body and your brain are on the same page and you achieve your goal: your goal of the finish line, of making a perfect piece of work.

A perfect piece of work is one that I can enjoy without an ounce of disapproval; a song that I can sing without wanting it to be different. A perfect piece of work is one that I am proud of.

The process to this point is very long, and sometimes unreachable, but in the instance that it has been reached, nothing excites me more.

Creativity is derived from a longing for something. Sometimes I write out of sheer boredom. But more times than not, I have words on the tip of my tongue – and to achieve their highest meaning, they need to be expressed in a song.

Susanne Wawra

Poet

DREAMER IN A DEAD LANGUAGE

Running on a roof of fish

slipping on a sandpaper saddle

tumbling down vinegar stairs

breaking through a window of salt

spiralling up a tornado of Q-tips

sitting down on a meadow of flies

scratching his bubblegum head

wondering what this dream

is trying to say.

Dòl Eoin MacKinnon

Filmmaker and Songwriter

NO PRETENTIOUS WAFFLE

For your information, I just deleted the 754 words worth of pretentious waffle I began with. That was my first attempt to respond to the questions posed, and part of the creative process. In actual fact, I don't understand the creative 'process' very well at all. I understand biological and physical processes much better than I do mental ones. Perhaps that's why sometimes the process is more important than the product of creativity.

I once had the privilege of engaging in a creative 'jam' with a woman suffering with Alzheimer's. She could play harmonica well and knew the tunes she learned years ago inside out, despite not being able to articulate how she felt, or know that the friendly strangers around her were her family. I insisted on playing four chords for her to make a tune up to. She struggled to begin with. It made her sigh; it made her laugh; it made her angry. And it made her try. Eventually she contrived a tune, a narrative, which navigated its way through the soundscape. And that made me incredibly happy. It was a forgettable tune, but a memorable process.

I remember I saw a grandmother pushing her grandson down the street and thinking... young people cry because they have experienced so little; old people cry because they have experienced so much.

I don't think one can begin a creative life anymore than one could dictate when they were created. You're born with it, it's nurtured (or tortured), and then eventually enough water and warmth germinate it in you. And that's when you can frantically shoot up through the darkness, see the light, make use of it, and grow bigger and bigger. However, eventually that process can mentally stabilise you to the point where you no longer feel the need for it. And the chances are you won't rate your own art as much as you used to.

I suppose the whole thing is a relationship, not a 'life'. You have to work at relationships or else they grow stale and you don't have as much sex as you used to. Perhaps you don't mind. If you want reassurance, comfort and safety, creativity is definitely not for you. If you have none of those things, then I hope at the very least you are creating something.

The stories I'm conceiving or trying to tell usually dictate my routine. It's 2:48 a.m.

If you enjoyed making up a story, and someone else enjoyed being told it, then keep telling stories. If you didn't enjoy my story, then that's just down to personal taste, obviously.

We are all dying to create. Some people leave behind bits of their DNA, some people leave behind popular things they made. Sometimes those people are the same person.

I haven't edited what I've written, and I would never not do that to anything meaningful I was to create. Ah heck, Da Vinci said he regretted never finishing one piece of work. Dream on. Treat this as a conversation with an egomaniac who hasn't even asked you who you are yet.

Who are you? Attempt to understand yourself, your behaviour and your situation better. In other words: create.

Marcas Mac an Tuairneir

Poet

CLOUDS

I stood on the doorstep,
Grappling with viridity,
To draw it into the house.

To suck in some novelty
To the chasm of my wits.
Churning
knows
     no
        repose.

Out there, before me,
The cloudy purview flowing
Pale
mauve,
    forever
       moving.

That zoetrope of being;
The boiling repetition,
Bellicose
turning
     of my
      life.

I am waiting for a letter,
That I never did send,
To reach its destination.

Cheryl Traylor

Creative Writer

VIRGINIA WOOLF: CREATIVE WRITING TEACHER

I recently spent many months inside Virginia Woolf's head. Okay, maybe not literally inside her head, but I did dig deep into her diaries, novels, and essays in an attempt to figure out what made this literary genius a literary genius. As you may imagine, my time there was intense, complex, and enlightening. I now know more about her creative process and the methods that she employed to become one of the most significant literary figures of the 20th century. While my writing is still nowhere near as eloquent and psychologically perceptive as Woolf's, I did glean some beneficial insight into her mode of creativity that I try to bring to my own creative life now.

1. *Find your pack.*

Although creativity is an intensely personal and individual endeavour, the creative process is enhanced by a group. In Woolf's case, this group was largely the Bloomsbury Group. The Bloomsberries, as they were also known, were a tightly knit, albeit loosely connected, group of friends and relatives that surrounded her throughout her life. From her teen years until the end of her days, Woolf had companions who were interested in a myriad of subjects: science, mythology, Freudian psychology, painting, art criticism, and writing. She was able to use her friends' expertise to enhance her writing. She also bounced her writing ideas off her friends through letters and long conversations. She listened and took their suggestions seriously, although she always had the final say in her work.

Find your writing group, literary *famiglia*, or poetry pack! Whatever you want to call it, find kindred spirits who will help you along the way by listening, giving constructive criticism, providing encouragement, and celebrating your successes. The creative process is not a safe, easy, linear path; it is a circuitous prowling down a dark and dangerous back alley at 3 am. You best have a few loyal fellow travellers who will have your back.

2. *Read. Read a lot.*

Reading is essential if one is to become a successful and innovative writer, and Woolf strived intensely to be both. As a young girl, she assigned herself strenuous reading lists and borrowed books from the extensive library of her father, the distinguished literary critic and author, Sir Leslie Stephen. As an adult she performed similar literary experiments on accomplished authors in much the same way that I did with her writing. She dissected the author's writing process to discover what exactly made that particular book work so perfectly. After reading Proust, she wrote to fellow Bloomsbury Group member, Roger Fry, 'But Proust so titillates my own desire for expression that I can hardly set out the sentence. Oh if I could write like that! I cry... I feel I *can* write like that, and seize my pen and then I *can't* write like that... it becomes an obsession.'[5] In a letter to her good friend, Ethel Smyth, Woolf wrote, 'Sometimes I

---

[5] Virginia Woolf, *The Letters of Virginia Woolf*, ed. Nigel Nicolson and Joanne Trautmann, vol. 2, (New York: Harvest-HBJ, 1976), 525.

think heaven must be one continuous unexhausted reading.'[6] She kept detailed journals filled with reading notes, newspaper clippings, and scraps of paper that she jotted when she did not have her notebook handy.

Read, read, and read! Read broadly from all genres. Also, keep a reading notebook and take detailed notes as you read. Note interesting passages, page numbers, and anything that catches your eye and makes you think. Did I mention: *read*?

3. *Get outside and walk in nature.*

Walking in nature stirs the creative juices. Woolf was known to walk many hours a day on the downs near her home in Sussex. Her niece, Henrietta Garnett, said that Virginia walked in the cold, rain, and snow. Walking in nature was an impetus to her writing; it cleared her mind and allowed space for her stories to grow and evolve. She, like her father, would speak aloud stories that came to mind during her forays. She found nature not only in the country, but also right in London. She wrote about her park wanderings in her thought-provoking short story, 'Kew Gardens'. Nature is a common theme running through Woolf's writings — from the seashore to parks to orchards, she brings the natural world into her writing. Being in nature was very important to her and to her Bloomsbury Group friends. (This little piece of information transformed into my Master's thesis.)

Go for walks to bring some fresh air into your body and your

---

[6] Woolf, *The Letters of Virginia Woolf*, ed. Nigel Nicolson and Joanne Trautmann, vol. 5, (New York: Harvest-HBJ 1979), 319.

writing. It is easy to get stuck in a writing rut and not be able to dig your way out when you need a change of scenery. Take walks on community greenways or in city parks. Arboretums are perfect havens of nature that are tucked away into city squares, usually near universities. When time permits, take longer hikes through county, state, and national parks. Nothing stirs the soul like a radiant crimson sunset, a rollicking river, or a multicolored, autumnal, leaf-strewn path. A stirred soul leads to stirred senses, which leads to stirred creativity. *Voilà!*

4. *Write. Write a lot.*

And lastly, but unquestionably most important, to become a writer, one must actually write—a lot. Woolf and her husband, Leonard, were known to spend hours every morning writing, without exception. She was not one to welcome distractions from her writing, even visits from family and friends. She was also intensely interested in innovative writing. She experimented freely with different writing styles: stream-of-consciousness, mood pieces resembling post-impressionistic paintings, fake biographies, satire, and more. Woolf did not play it safe; she was constantly testing out new ideas.

In one well-known quote, she speaks out against conforming. Certainly this applies to writing as well; to create one must step out, risk failure, and break the chains on creative conformity. Writing in *The Common Reader*, she advises:

Once conform, once do what other people do because they do
it, and a lethargy steals over all the finer nerves and faculties
of the soul. She becomes all outer show and inward emptiness;

dull, callous, and indifferent.[7]

Woolf was anything but a conformist, especially when it came to writing. She was a multifaceted individual who knew what she wanted to do and did it. She wanted to write, so she wrote.

To be a writer, one must write. Every day. Even on days that you are too tired, too sick, too hopeless. If you want to write, you have to sit down with your computer or notebook and pen. There are many methods to create stories, novels, or essays, but they all involve putting fingers to keys or pen to paper. There is no getting around this one. A writing instructor once told me that the only people who should be writing are the ones who cannot help but do so. Writers write because they have to. Do you *have* to write? Yes? Do it!

On an unseasonably warm October morning while I was in Rodmell near Woolf's English country home, Monk's House, I read a passage from *Orlando* in which Woolf perfectly describes the arduous task of writing.

> Anyone moderately familiar with the rigours of
> composition will not need to be told the rest of the story
> in detail; how he wrote it and it seemed good;   read it and
> it seemed vile; corrected and tore up; cut out; put in; was
> in ecstasy; in despair; had his good nights and bad
> mornings; snatched at ideas and lost them; saw his book
> plain before him and it vanished; acted his people's parts
> as he ate; mouthed them as he walked; now cried; now

---

[7] Woolf, *The Common Reader*, (Orlando: Harvest-Harcourt, 1984), 61.

laughed; vacillated between this style and that; now preferred the heroic and pompous; next the plain and simple; now the vales of Tempe; then the fields of Kent or Cornwall; and could not decide whether he was the divinest genius or the greatest fool in the world.[8]

Later that evening as I retraced Woolf's final steps along the River Ouse, I recalled the passage. I stopped as it suddenly dawned on me: my literary heroine, the writer I had placed on a marble pedestal, was a mere human. She struggled with self-doubt, obsessed over creating nothing less than perfection, and had her share of critics, of whom she herself was the most brutal. And yet she created her work—her breathtaking, heart-stopping, ear-pleasing work. Her writing was not only her work; it was her life. She produced classics that have stood the test of time, because she was dedicated to her craft. She wrote because she was a writer.

And so I try to incorporate Woolf's creative methods into my life. I read (too much), walk (often), write (too little), and am constantly looking for my pack (and trying to embrace my vulnerability so that I will share my writing with others). Overall, I'm getting there, wherever there is. I'm making my way and trying to enjoy the journey—this journey of my life, my creative life. Thank you, Virginia Woolf, for being my teacher.

---

[8] Woolf, *Orlando*, (Read Books Ltd., 2012), 70.

Annie Higgen

Poet

TO WRITE

to stare

to hesitate

to think

to wish

to push

to tear

to throw

to pick

to quip

to try

to smile

to glow

to hold

to catch

to keep

to draw

to tend

to long

to love

to bite

To fight

To test

To sooth

To write

BIBLIOGRAPHY

Garnett, Henrietta, personal interview with Cheryl Traylor, 29 Oct. 2013.

Homer, *Iliad*, trans. Robert Fagles, (New York City: Penguin, 1990).

Pratchett, Terry, *Hogfather*, (Gollancz, 1996).

Pressfield, Stephen, *The War of Art: Break Through the Blocks and Win Your Inner Creative Battles*, (New York: Black Irish Entertainment LLC, 2002).–

'You as the Muse Sees You', *Stephen Pressfield Online*, (9 Oct. 2013), (17 April 2015), <http://www.stevenpressfield.com/2013/10/you-as-the-muse-sees-you>.

Woolf, Virginia, *Orlando*, (Read Books Ltd., 2012).

Woolf, Virginia, *The Letters of Virginia Woolf*, Ed. Nigel Nicolson and Joanne Trautmann, Vol. 2, (New York: Harvest-HBJ, 1976).

Woolf, Virginia, *The Letters of Virginia Woolf*, Ed. Nigel Nicolson and Joanne Trautmann., Vol. 5., (New York: Harvest-HBJ, 1979).

Woolf, Virginia, *The Common Reader*, (Orlando: Harvest-Harcourt, 1984).

CONTRIBUTORS

Caleb Ackley is a photographer local to the San Diego area. While photography is his passion, he tends to abandon all for the sake of pie.

Lisa Jane Birch is a practicing fine artist and a graduate of Duncan of Jordanstone College of Art and Design in Dundee, Scotland. Her work primarily consists of abstract drawings with pen, reflections of personal thought and mental dialogue.

Matt Bishop is lead guitar and vocals for the indie folk/chamber pop band, Hey Marseilles. Hey Marseilles is based in Seattle, Washington and has been featured by NPR, KEXP, and *Seattle Weekly*.

Seth Brown is the pianist of Why I Must Be Careful, an experimental rock band based in Portland, Oregon.

Bart Budwig grew up on the Idaho Palouse, with a pawnshop trumpet and a heart as big as a skyscraper - if skyscrapers knew how to be humble. Bart learned melody from classic jazz charts, and learned that fault-lines in big hearts create drifting continents, cut new oceans and forge new mountains. Everyone close to him disappeared, whether to death or Texas, and from Texas he got a letter from Waylon Jennings entreating him to pick up a guitar and a pen.

Tracy Butler is a visual artist who works both digitally and in chalk pastel. Formerly, she painted murals for private individuals and companies, but now she concentrates on wildlife. She has held successful solo and joint exhibitions in London, Glasgow, and at the Pittenweem Arts Festival; her work can be seen in galleries throughout Scotland and England. Tracy has worked for the Royal National Theatre in London and Edinburgh and is currently on the set of the TV series *Outlander*.

Michelle Case writes music in her spare time. She has been writing for eight years and leads music for her church and for Younglife. Her favourite time to write is when she's with her cousin, Mary Claire Miltenberger. They mix their influences and styles and write together. Michelle is in high school and lives in Dallas, TX.

Nichola Deadman was born in South Africa. She studied Political Science at the University of Pretoria before moving to Japan to teach English. She is currently enrolled in the University of Glasgow's MLitt Creative Writing programme. She enjoys crochet, cooking, and reminiscing about when she had time to do either.

Colin Herd is a poet, fiction writer and critic based in Edinburgh. His poetry includes *too ok* (collection, BlazeVOX, 2011), *like* (pamphlet, Knives, Forks and Spoons Press, 2011), and *Glovebox* (collection, Knives Forks and Spoons Press, 2013), which was highly commended by the Forward Prizes, 2014. He has published over 60 reviews and articles on art and literature in publications including *Aesthetica Magazine*, *3:AM Magazine*, *PN:Review* and *The Independent*, and has read and performed his work widely.

Annie Higgen is a Glasgow-based poet and sound artist. Previously working as a singer-songwriter, she gradually moved to poetry and more experimental sound art and finished her MA in Poetic Practice at Royal Holloway in 2014. Annie is particularly interested in exploring concepts of place within social and political frameworks, but she also enjoys more traditional page-based poetry. Her newest project is a year-long blog based on the *Norton Anthology of Postmodern American Poetry*.

Emma Jane Kimmell creates art for those who see old things as a part of something new, for those who see black and white as distinctly colourful, for those who see magic in reality, and she makes art for the sake of art. With this lens, Seattle based artist and children's art instructor Emma Jane fashions her cheerfully quirky style into prints, paintings, and little people.

Barry Lategan is one of the UK's most renowned and influential photographers, best known for his early discovery and portraits of the supermodel Twiggy – two of which are exhibited in the V&A Museum. Lategan has photographed some of the most notable celebrities of the past forty years, including HRH Princess Anne, Paul and Linda McCartney, Calvin Klein, Margaret Thatcher, and Salmon Rushdie, among others. His work has been featured on the front covers of *Vogue* and *Harper's Bazaar*.

Ian Lyles (drums) and **Aaron Pomerantz** (dobro, mandolin) are musicians and members of the indie folk rock band, Weinland (Badman, Jealous Butcher Records, Woodphone Records). Weinland is based in Portland, Oregon and has been featured on *Paste*, *Entertainment Weekly*, and *USA Today*.

Dòl Eoin MacKinnon is a singer-songwriter, filmmaker and actor from the Isle of Harris. He has produced and directed documentaries, music videos, corporate videos, and is currently writing two dramas and recording two albums with his band, Macanta.

Kerrie McKinnel is a mum and an MLitt Creative Writing student at the University of Glasgow. Between dealing with toddler tantrums and one-word-a-page board books, she enjoys reading, walking and baking. Her fiction writing is inspired by her experiences of motherhood, and the occasional fleeting memory of what life used to be like when her home was quiet and did not smell like nappies and milk. She lives in Scotland with her husband and son.

Sean Ogilvie is a singer and songwriter who plays for the indie folk band, Musée Mécanique (Frogstand Records). Musée Mécanique is based in Portland, Oregon and has been featured by *Pitchfork Media* and NPR's *All Things Considered*.

Sarah Palmer is a creative writing student on the MLitt programme at the University of Glasgow.

Ian Richardson lives on the East coast of Scotland and has been reading books for years. Eventually, inevitably, he started writing. The first short story he ever wrote won a competition but he's not been able to maintain that 100% success rate. He recently had an e-book published. Ian loves exploring writing genres, drinks a lot of coffee, doesn't sleep much and is currently supposed to be working on a new novel.

Justin Ringle is a singer and songwriter for the band Horse Feathers (Lucky Madison, Kill Rock Stars), an indie folk band based in Portland, Oregon. Horse Feathers has been featured by *Billboard* and NPR.

Lovísa Elísabet Sigrúnardóttir is an Icelandic singer and songwriter who creates an enchanting blend of indie blues and folk by the name of her alter ego, Lay Low (Cod Music). Lay Low has won several awards and has been featured on *iTunes* as 'one of the best discoveries of 2008.'

Javier Suarez is a singer and songwriter who attended the Liverpool Institute of Performing Arts. He formerly created music with the Washington-based indie folk band, Yarn Owl, and now plays with the synth pop group, Gathered Ghosts.

Brandon Summers is lead vocals and guitar for the alternative rock duo, The Helio Sequence (Sub Pop Records). The Helio Sequence is based in Portland, Oregon and has been featured by *Stereogum* and *BrooklynVegan*.

Cheryl Traylor is a word lover and reading addict who lives life as a perpetual spiritual journey. Her body lives with her best friends in a too-big city on a too-tiny urban plot, but her spirit dwells among the oaks and wild blackberries. On the best of days, she puts pen to paper and attempts to create a world with more love and less mediocrity. Other days, she surfs the net and plays on Facebook.

Jennifer Trovato is a photographer who lives in Maryland with her husband, fellow photographer Horace Trovato, and their two children. Horace and Jennifer enjoy shooting film and pursuing projects that tell a great story. You can find them at horaceandmaephotography.tumblr.com.

Marcas Mac an Tuairneir writes poetry, prose, drama and journalism in Gaelic and English. His début collection, *Deò*, was published in 2013 by Grace Note Publications. A second, *Lus na Tùise*, is expected from the same in 2015 as is his début novel from Acair. In 2014, he was awarded the Highland Literary Salon prize for poetry and came both second and first place in the Baker Prize for Gaelic Writing.

Forrest VanTuyl (An American Forrest) grew up in a hundred-year-old farmhouse in rural southwestern Washington, started writing songs at fifteen, and started riding horses at twenty-five. Between touring, chasing songs,and seasonal employment, Forrest hasn't lived anywhere more than six months in the last four years, and doesn't speak Spanish as well as he should, or very well at all, really.

Susanne Wawra is a German visual artist and poet based in Dublin, Ireland. After an exploration of business in an international big name company, she decided to swap a secure career for life as an artist. Even though English is not her mother tongue, it is her preferred medium for poetry. Recent publications include *Weyfarers*, *Valve Journal*, *The Galway Review*, *Boyne Berries* and *The Glad Rag*.

Stuart White is a Scottish author, currently studying the MLitt Creative Writing course at Glasgow University. School Teacher by day, writer of fantasy worlds by night, he is the co-author of two Biology textbooks. Strike up a conversation about *Star Wars* or *Lord of the Rings* and he's all yours... seriously!

Jo Young served in the British Army for seventeen years before retiring to spend more time with her two young sons. She simultaneously rediscovered the joy of writing, having done very little of it since winning a short story competition back in 1998. She plans to keep going this time.

ABOUT THE EDITOR

Molly Miltenberger Murray is the author of *Today, She Is* (Wipf and Stock, 2013), a creative non-fiction account of recovery from traumatic brain injury, and is editor of the blog and book, *The Atelier Project* (2015). She has written and edited for *Artist Reformation* and has been published by *Edge* and *The Stanza Blog*. She is pursuing her MLitt in Creative Writing from the University of Glasgow from her home in the Scottish Highlands, where she lives with her husband, Gordon, and their cat, the Great Catsby.

Molly creates best when she has worked out, stretched, taken a long walk, and the house is reasonably clean. When she writes she likes to light a candle, smell something delicious, turn on calming indie folk like Musée Mécanique, and hide in her very own atelier with a mug of iced coffee or vanilla rooibos tea. She keeps postcards of her favorite places on her desk. She likes colour on her fingernails (usually something in the blue range).

Molly finds it natural to write poetry and creative non-fiction, and is working on creating fiction.

www.ingramcontent.com/pod-product-compliance
Lightning Source LLC
Chambersburg PA
CBHW070904180526
45168CB00005B/1929